Contents

Who was Auguste Rodin?

Auguste Rodin
was a French artist
and **sculptor**. He
is most famous for
the **statues** of
people he made
out of clay, **bronze**,
and **marble**.

The Life and Work of
Auguste Rodin

Richard Tames

Heinemann Library
Chicago, Illinois

Customer Service 888-454-2279
Visit our website at www.heinemannraintree.com

Designed by Jo Malivoire and Q2A Creative
Printed in China by South China Printing Company

10 09 08 07 06
10 9 8 7 6 5 4 3 2 1

New edition ISBN: 1-40348-488-0 (hardcover)
                1-40348-499-6 (paperback)

The Library of Congress has cataloged the first edition as follows:
Tames, Richard
        Auguste Rodin / Richard Tames.
            p. cm. — (The life and work of–)
        Includes bibliographical references and index.
        Summary: Briefly examines the life and work of the French sculptor, describing and giving examples of his art
        ISBN 1-57572-342-5 (lib. bdg.)
        1. Rodin. Auguste, 1840-1917 Juvenile literature. 2. Sculptors-
-France-Biography-Juvenile literature. [1. Rodin. Auguste,
1840-1917. 2. Sculptors 3. Art appreciation.] I. Title. II. Series.

NB553.R7 T34   2000
730'. 92—dc21   00-025786
[B]

_Acknowledgments
The author and publishers are grateful to the following for permission to reproduce copyright material: Bridgeman Art Library: Musee d'Orsay, Paris p. 21; Musée Rodin, Paris: pp. 4, 6, 14, 20, Hélène Moulonguet p. 7, Adam Rzepka pp. 5, 9, 13, 18, 25, Charles Aubry pp. 10,12, Erik and Petra Hesmerg p. 11, Bruno Jarret p. 15, Jessie Lipscomb p. 16, Jêrome Manoukian pp. 17, 23, Pierre Bonnard p. 22, Edward Steichen 24, Choumoff p. 28, Jean de Calan p. 29; Photo RMN: R G Ojeda p. 19; Roger-Viollet: Harlingue-Viollet p. 26; Trip: Christopher Rennie p. 27

Cover photograph: *Jules Dalou* by Auguste Rodin, reproduced with permission of AKG Images.

The publishers would like to thank Nancy Harris for her assistance in the preparation of this book.

Some words in this book are in bold, **like this.** You can find out what they mean by looking in the Glossary.

Auguste tried to show feelings in his **sculptures**. The people in this sculpture are unhappy because their city in France has been taken over by an English king.

Early Years

Auguste was born in Paris, France on November 12 1840. This is a photograph of Auguste at the age of nine with his mother. He started drawing when he was 10 years old.

Auguste went to a special drawing school
when he was 14. Here are some of his
drawings. He began to make clay models
at the age of 15. His **sculptures** were
based on his drawings of people.

Hard Times

Auguste began to earn money making stone decorations for buildings. When his sister died in 1862, he was very sad and he tried to become a **monk**. But he soon returned to his work.

Auguste made art for other people during the day. But he worked on his own models in the evenings. He was only 19 when he made this **sculpture** of his father.

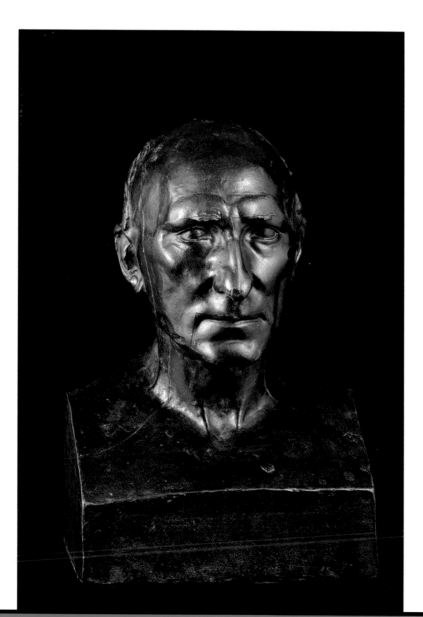

Great Changes

In 1864, when he was 24, Auguste met Rose Beuret. She **posed** for him and was his helper for the rest of his life. Auguste got his first **studio**. It was a cold, damp stable.

Auguste and Rose had a son, named
Auguste, in 1866. Auguste made this **bust** of
a young woman the year after he met Rose.
It is called *Young Woman in a Flowered Hat.*

Leaving Paris

Auguste needed to earn money to feed his family. He went to work in Belgium. In 1875 he went to Italy for a year. He **studied** the work of the **sculptor** Michelangelo.

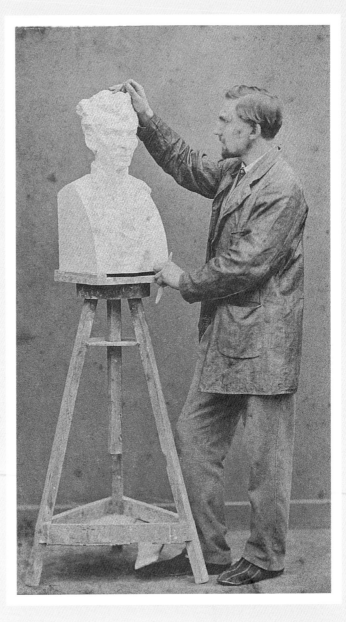

Auguste wanted to become famous. But his *Man with the Broken Nose* was turned down for an important **exhibition**. Many people did not like Auguste's realistic style.

Fame at last

Auguste started to become famous when he was almost 40 years old. His work could bring him trouble too. He made a life-size statue of a soldier. It was called *Age of Bronze*.

Age of Bronze looked so real that some people said Auguste cheated. After this, he made his statues bigger or smaller than real life. This proved he did not cheat.

The Work of a Lifetime

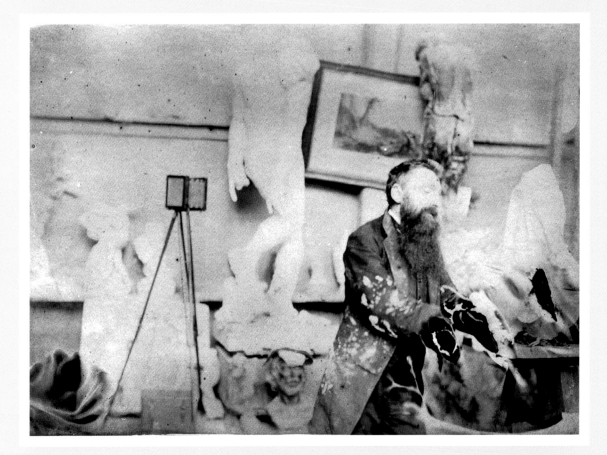

In 1880 Auguste was asked to make a huge doorway for a museum in Paris. He based his drawings for it on the way the Italian poet Dante described Hell. It was called *The Gates of Hell*.

Auguste's most famous **statue**, *The Thinker*, is meant to be Dante. It was meant to go on the top of *The Gates of Hell.*

Camille

This **bust** of Auguste was made by the **sculptor** Camille Claudel in 1888. Auguste liked the bust very much. Camille helped Auguste with his work. She also **posed** for him.

Camille posed for this **sculpture**. It is called *Thought*. Auguste made it in 1888. In it Camille is wearing a hat usually worn by brides in northern France.

A Big Studio

Auguste moved to Meudon, near Paris. Here he had a big new **studio** with lots of space. He often had up to 50 helpers there. They made **carvings** from his clay models.

Auguste loved to read. He got a lot
of ideas from books. In 1897 he made
this **bust** of the great French writer
Victor Hugo.

Famous Faces

Auguste liked making **busts** of his friends or people he wanted to thank. This picture shows him making a bust of the French **sculptor** Jean Alexandre Falguière.

Auguste showed this **statue** of the French writer Honoré de Balzac in 1898. Auguste read Balzac's books so he could understand Balzac better.

Success

In 1900 Auguste had his first big **exhibition** in Paris. It included over 150 of his **sculptures**. People came from all over the world to see his work.

Auguste called this sculpture *The Cathedral*. He thought that the two hands raised together looked like the pointed arches in cathedrals.

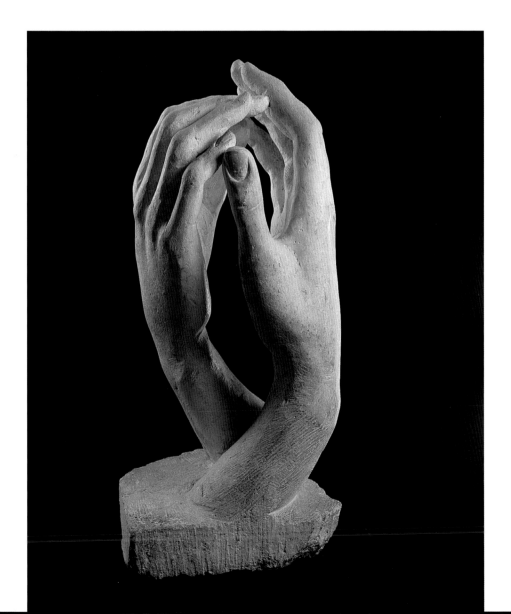

Home and Museum

In 1903 Auguste had a **biography** written about him. It was by the German poet Rainer Maria Rilke. This picture shows Rainer with Rose and Auguste and their dogs outside their house.

Rainer invited Auguste to the Hotel Biron in Paris. This building became Auguste's home. Today it is a museum. Many people come here to see Auguste's work.

Last Days

Rose died on February 14 1917. Auguste died on November 17 1917. They were buried together at Meudon under a copy of Auguste's **statue** of *The Thinker*.

When Auguste died, *The Gates of Hell* was still unfinished. It can be seen at the Rodin Museum in Paris.

Timeline

1840	Rene-Francois-Auguste Rodin is born on November 12.
1854	Auguste goes to drawing school.
1857	Auguste fails to get into art college.
1862–63	Auguste tries to become a **monk**.
1864	Auguste meets Rose Beuret.
1870	Auguste joins the army.
1871	Auguste leaves the army and moves to Belgium.
1875–76	Auguste travels in Italy to **study** art.
1877	Auguste moves back to Paris.
1880	Auguste is asked to make *The Gates of Hell*.
1897	Auguste moves to Meudon.
1900	Auguste shows 150 **sculptures** at a Paris **exhibition**.
1903	Rainer Maria Rilke writes Auguste's **biography**.
1914–18	World War I.
1917	Auguste dies on November 17.

Glossary

biography story of a person's life

bronze metal made of tin and copper

bust statue of a head and shoulders

carvings object cut into a shape

cathedral large church, usually in a city

exhibition public showing of art

marble special kind of limestone rock

monk man who devotes his whole life to his religion

pose to stand or sit in a certain way while an artist paints or draws you

sculptor person who carves wood or stone to make works of art

sculpture statue or carving

statue carved, molded, or sculpted figure of a person or animal

studio place where an artist works

study to learn about a subject

More Books to Read

Wolfe, Gillian. *Oxford First Book of Art.* New York: OUP, 2004.

Tames, Richard. *The Life and Work of Michelangelo Buonarroti.* Chicago: Heinemann Library, 2006.

More Sculptures to See

Balzac in a Frock Coat, 1891. Museum of Modern Art, New York City, NY.

Brother and Sister, (plaster created in 1890). Museum of Fine Arts, Boston, Mass.

Index